INVITATION TO HAIRSPLITTING

A hypercritical investigation into the true function of the
Warren Commission and the true nature
of the Warren Report

by

Jacques ZWART, M. Sc.
Member MENSA International

Paris Amsterdam

This is a reprint of the book written by our late uncle Jaap (Jacques) Zwart. It was originally published by Paris Amsterdam, which appears to be non-existent anymore. Jaap transferred the copyrights of this (and other works) to the children of his youngest brother, Simon Zwart. We did our best contact the original publisher, but in vain. If you have any information on the legacy of the original publisher, please do not hesitate to contact us at legacy_jaap@zwart.nl

Enschede, October 13th, 2020

This book is dedicated to the memory of
- the late President John F. Kennedy, of whom not one further word
  need be said;
- the late Senator Robert F. Kennedy, whom I regret to this day not
  having informed of my findings when meeting him shortly before
  his assassination;
- the late Allen W. Dulles, for many years my highest-level
  supervisor, who more than any other member of the Warren
  Commission helped me, by his remarks at Commission hearings,
  solve the riddle of the Warren Report;
- the late Lee Harvey Oswald, rightly called 'the unsung hero of this
  episode' by his mother, who regrettably did not cooperate with
  those erecting a monument to his heroism.

It could not have been written without the invaluable work of all
previous critics of the Warren Report, nor without the devoted efforts,
unrecognized so far, of all those who were willing to follow the
Warren Commission on its path and help it reach its goal.

Of them, I particularly wish to mention, and express my
indebtedness to, Mr. Albert Jenner, Mr. William Coleman, Mr. Robert
Oswald, and Mr. William McKenzie, as I have come to know them
through my scrutiny of the Warren Commission's publications.

Last not least, I am deeply appreciative of the US Information Center
('Amerika-Haus') in Frankfurt/Main, Germany, and the charming
ladies on its staff for their manifold assistance, competent advice and
kind cooperation.

JACQUES ZWART

The Hague, Holland
November 12, 1970

*'Certainly you ought to have some
confidence in a commission that
is appointed by the President'*

*'We are here to do justice and be
fair to everyone concerned in
this matter'*

Admonitions by Commission
chairman Earl Warren to
Mrs. Marguerite Oswald

Table of Contents

List of Illustrations:

1. Executive Order No. 11130 (White House Press Release of November 30, 1963; Appendix I to the Warren Report)

2. White House Press Release of November 29, 1963 (Appendix II to the Warren Report)

3. Letter of Transmittal of the Warren Report

4. Title Page of a 'Final Report' to the US Department of Health, Education, and Welfare

5. Part of the Letter of Transmittal of the same 'Final Report'

6. Official Photograph of the Presentation of the Warren Commission's Report to President Johnson on Sept. 24, 1964

7. Title Page of one of the Volumes of 'Hearings and Exhibits'

8. Title Page of the Warren Report

   (N.B.: Underlinings and framings in the illustrations are the author's)

I. The Continuing Assassination Mystery

Whatever else the assassination of President John F. Kennedy on November 22, 1963 in Dallas, Texas may have been (and of course it was plenty), it originally was a *mystery* only in the sense that any homicide perpetrated by a person intent on concealing his guilt challenges its investigators with a mystery of sorts - a mystery which in the 'mystery thrillers' they then hasten to clear up.

Given the circumstances of the assassination and the person of the victim, the chances of clearing up this particular mystery were of course incomparably better than average. The President had been murdered while on a public tour, in full daylight, in the presence of hundreds of witnesses and dozens of law-enforcing officials, including the highest local ones, who thus were able to start their criminal investigation before the President had even expired.

Within an hour, a second homicide (that of Police Officer Tippit), evidently connected with the assassination of the President, had come to join it, and here, too, the circumstances were most auspicious for speedy clarification: plain daylight and numerous eyewitnesses, this time not only to the dying of the victim but even to the shooting by the killer. By all standards, both homicides should normally have ceased to be mysteries within a minimum of time.

It therefore could surprise no one that before another hour had passed a suspect, Lee Harvey Oswald, was picked up who appeared to have had both the *means* and the *opportunity* to commit both murders. As to his *motive*, in the case of Officer Tippit it could be presumed to be his wish to escape arrest, while in the President's case it seemed to follow from Oswald's apparently clear-cut leftist leanings and background (defection to and several years of residence in the Soviet Union, marriage to a Soviet citizen, subscription to leftist US and Russian publications, pronounced activity in and on behalf of the Fair Play for Cuba Committee, etc.).

Hence, even before the assassination day had drawn to a close, the State of Texas was all set to arraign Oswald, besides for shooting Officer Tippit, for 'assassinating the President of the United States as part of an international conspiracy'.[1]

At this point, however, the smoothly running official machinery for clearing up the Dallas homicides began to develop trouble. The suspect steadfastly denied both killings, even any form of involvement in them. After much telephoning between, of all places, the White House and the Texas authorities,[2] the reference to an 'international conspiracy' was dropped from the arraignment of Oswald, who thus with respect to President Kennedy was solely indicted for homicide with malice aforethought.

Now it was at this stage of the proceedings, and after the competent Dallas authorities (Homicide Bureau Chief Capt. *Fritz*, Police Chief *Curry*, District Attorney *Wade*) had for several days impressed the public (on TV) and the information media (in press conferences) with revelations of rapidly accumulating evidence 'cinching' Oswald as the President's assassin, that Oswald, while still in police Custody and even on police premises, was unexpectedly shot by a gate-crasher - nightclub operator Jack Ruby. This well-nigh unbelievable development constituted of course a mystery in its own right.

The result, besides worldwide consternation, was the abandoning on that very same day of every possibility to have the assassination mystery clarified by ordinary criminological and legal means. For Dallas District Attorney Wade, having already got rid of the 'conspiracy' involvement and now of course physically unable to go on prosecuting Oswald, publicly declared himself fully satisfied that he had had the right man, the man who had single-handedly killed both President Kennedy and Officer Tippit, so that under these new circumstances, with no suspect being alive and none expected to be, it was both proper and lawful for him to declare both cases closed. (Interestingly, in taking this momentous decision the

---

[1] Cf. 5 H 218-219 (i.e. Volume 5 of the Warren Commission's Hearings and Exhibits, p. 218-219), Henry *Wade*.

[2] Cf. 5 H 259-260 (Waggoner *Carr*).

District Attorney did not even await the results and pictures of the President's autopsy, conducted two days earlier at Bethesda Naval Hospital, which upon competent criminological interpretation might very well have either strongly supported or totally disproved his professed opinion that the President had been killed by a single assassin).

The mystery by now evidently had become a man-sized one, and moreover one no longer solvable by ordinary process of law, To have it cleared up nevertheless, President Johnson within a matter of days created and appointed what was to become known as the *Warren Commission*.

* *
*

On November 29, 1963, one week after the assassination, President Johnson announced the creation of the 'Warren Commission'; on September 28, 1964 the Commission's so-called 'Warren Report' was made public and the Commission itself dissolved. The intermediate 10-month period appears, in retrospect, to have been the only one in which a halfway satisfactory situation existed with regard to the assassination mystery.

True, the Dallas mysteries were as unsolved as ever, but 7 persons of high station and unquestioned integrity gifted with eminently qualified minds and armed with unprecedented authority were looking into all of them, and the findings of these men would be made known to the public. And when the 'Warren Report' eventually was published, appreciable segments of the national and international public did indeed believe that the mysteries had been largely clarified - if not in every detail, then at least in substance.

As we all know, this situation has not lasted. Numerous students, some with little if any less brilliant minds than the Commissioners' if not with the same station in life, have pored over the 'Warren Report' and found it wanting in innumerable respects. The picture presented by the Report was found to be at variance:

* *with logic and common sense*, e.g. where it postulated a 'magic bullet' (Exhibit 399), virtually unscathed, yet supposedly having caused all of President Kennedy's and Governor Connally's wounds but for the President's lethal head wound;
* *with official reports not taken into consideration by the Commission*, e.g. the report prepared by the FBI agents assisting ex officio at the President's autopsy; and even
* *with the material presented by the Commission itself* in its famous '26 Volumes' of Hearings and Exhibits (published on November 23, 1964), as was pointed out e.g. by as illustrious a scholar as Oxford professor of history Hugh Trevor-Roper in his introduction to American author Mark Lane's *'Rush to Judgment'*.

Besides Professor Trevor-Roper and Mark Lane, the critics of the 'Warren Report' include such noted personalities as Los Angeles professor Richard H. Popkin *('The Second Oswald')*, Pulitzer Prize winner Sylvan Fox *('The Unanswered Questions about President Kennedy's Assassination')*, French correspondent Leo Sau-vage *('l' Affaire Oswald')*, Harvard scholar Edward Jay Epstein *('Inquest')* and many others in the USA and abroad. While the work of these authors certainly is not above severe criticism in numerous respects, it has, in the aggregate, achieved one invaluable and incontestable result: it has made the opinion untenable that the assassination mystery was solved by the 'Warren Report'. Anyone still clinging to that opinion is cherishing a mere illusion and undoubtedly has studied neither the Report, nor the works of its critics. To any serious student of the assassination these are mere truisms.

Thus the 'Warren Report', far from clarifying the assassination mystery, actually compounded it. For in addition to the still unsolved John F. Kennedy, Tippit and Oswald killings, we are now also faced with the mysterious fact that the Commission created and instructed by President Johnson to ascertain the truth about all three homicides instead presented the world, in its Final Report, with an account which does not stand up to competent scrutiny.

10

And even if this apparent failure to arrive at - or at least make known - the truth should be due to nothing more sinister than lack of time (as author *Epstein* has suggested), there is the further fact that the American government as a whole, and the former Commissioners as individuals (the Commission as a body having ceased to exist), is and are opposed to any reopening of the case. In defense of this stand the late Commissioner Allen W. Dulles has said with respect to the critics: 'If they've found another assassin, let them name names and supply the evidence' (a condition which the critics so far have indeed failed to meet), while it has also been asserted that 'not one shred of new evidence has been brought forth by anyone since the Warren Commission made its findings public which would merit... a new hearing.'

Now this is a statement which any thoughtful reader of both the Report and its critics is apt to question and deplore, especially since it came, in the form as quoted, from as uncontroversial a witness as President Kennedy's former press secretary Pierre Salinger (in his Preface to journalist Charles Roberts' *'The Truth about the Assassination'*, a work striking one as an all-out assault on the Warren Report critics).

The totality of the official refusal to reopen the case is amply illustrated by the following September 1969 episode: in a letter to Mr. Warren, Executive Director Fensterwald of a newly-formed private investigation committee comprising various well-known critics of the Warren Report requested the former Commission chairman to take cognizance of various documentary and photographic evidence assembled by the private committee with a view to a hoped-for reopening of the case. This letter Mr. Warren refused to accept or have accepted by his staff.[3]

---

[3] Committee to Investigate Assassinations, Washington, D.C., Progress Report After One Year of Existence, January 1970.

Undoubtedly a consistent stand, yet one only underlining that as this time, seven years after the assassination, we are still faced with the following mysteries:

1. What were the actual facts, manifestly not uncovered by the 'Warren Report', concerning the assassination of President Kennedy, the murder of Officer Tippit and the shooting of Lee Harvey Oswald?
2. Why did the President's official Commission to investigate these three homicides present, in its final report, an unacceptable account of each one of them?
3. Why do all demands for a reopening of the case, no matter by whom presented, meet with an official cold shoulder?

And to be complete, let us also ask this:
4. Given the inadequacy (to say the least) of the Warren Report, how was it possible for the late President's late brother RobertF. Kennedy to express 'complete satisfaction'[4] with the Report and for the late President's press secretary Pierre Salinger to assure that 'the Warren Commission performed a difficult assignment honorably and well, and that it accurately pinpointed the assassin of John F Kennedy'? [5]

Questions upon questions - and it is about time, seven years after the assassination, that satisfying, lucid answers should be found to them.

Precisely this is what the present book is about.

In the following chapters it will propose solutions, based on documentary evidence and not on speculations, to the above mysteries 2, 3 and 4, while pointing out a way in which the basic mystery package, no. 1, might be solved without reopening the case.

---

[4] New York Times, September 28, 1964.
[5] Charles Roberts: 'The Truth About the Assassination', preface by Pierre Salinger.

II. In Defense of Hairsplitting

In embarking on my analysis, it is my hope that the reader will find it marked by subtlety and precision, yet I very much fear that unless certain things are explained in advance he will find it marked by nothing else but uncalled-for and ridiculous hairsplitting. Any reader inclined to take this view is therefore requested to bear in mind the following four things.

First: it has been widely noted, and extensively commented upon, that all of the Commissioners and senior staff members of the Warren Commission were *lawyers*, including some of the most brilliant legal minds of America. Thus, when consulting the 'Warren Report' and the accompanying 26 volumes of Hearings and Exhibits (and let it be remarked right away that I shall draw conclusions from *no other material* than from these official documents) we are dealing with documents drawn up, interrogations conducted and exhibits selected by lawyers.

Now it may be considered well known that where- or whenever in life we are confronted with material authored, co-authored, inspired or otherwise influenced by lawyers, hence by persons trained to be sticklers for utmost precision, it is advisable, and indeed often even essential, to *consider and weigh every word* - to refuse to be satisfied with what the given document *appears* to say or to mean but to establish beyond a doubt what, in the final analysis, it *actually* says or means. Surely no member of the Warren Commission could possibly object to such an approach to its material, the sole procedure to make sure that we indeed are not missing any of the points the Commission may have intended to make.

Second: let it not be forgotten for a moment that in trying to arrive at the truth of the John F. Kennedy assassination and the 'Warren Report' we are treading most delicate ground. Let us be well aware of what we are doing. The single possible alternative to the Report's thesis of Lee Harvey Oswald's single-handed guilt is a conspiracy. For if Oswald did not act alone, he either acted together - hence conspired - with others, or he did not act at all. But in the latter case one has to replace him not only by another marksman but also by at least one person who planted the various clues pointing to the innocent Oswald (notably the 'magic bullet' found at Parkland Hospital in Dallas and undoubtedly fired from Oswald's rifle), so once again one ends up with a conspiracy. And in all of these cases the Warren Commission, which labored hard to produce a false report, appears to have been a party, though not to committing the assassination, but to concealing the truth about it.

Evidently these are all alternatives of the utmost gravity, and the very least we can do in trying to pinpoint the correct one is to keep a clear head and to painstakingly beware of jumping to unwarranted conclusions - with 'unwarranted' meaning in this case: not absolutely justified by unassailable fact, by impeccable logic and by reasoning of the strictest sort, the sort that is apt to strike less strict minds as hairsplitting.

Third: hairsplitting, or as I prefer it: the application of utmost precision may be the only way of finding out what, if anything, the Warren Commission wrote *between the lines* of the close to 20,000 pages left to us as its legacy.

It has been intimated, and often enough been charged outright, that the Warren Commission, whatever its ostensible function, in reality had the task of 'protecting the national interest', of 'dispelling damaging rumors' and of showing the world, in the words of Commissioner John J. McCloy, 'that America is not a banana republic, where a government can be changed by conspiracy',[6] all or any of which may of course well have been incompatible with an explicit presentation of the facts, depending on what they were.

But need these lofty purposes have been incompatible with an *implicit* presentation of these same facts, carefully hidden between the lines and extractable from them only by most meticulous analysis - or, if one so prefers, hairsplitting? Certainly not in the case of lines written by men as brilliant, knowledgeable and experienced as the Commissioners and their hand-picked staff. In other words: there exists a priori a real possibility

---

[6] All quotations from Edward Jay Epstein: *'Inquest'*, chapter 2: The Dominant Purpose.

that the Commission solved the 'dilemma' of its 'dualism in purpose'[7] in a manner worthy of the intellectual prowess at its disposal - while *seemingly* depicting the assassination as a lone act by a lone, demented killer without conspiratorial connections, thus 'protecting the national interest' at least for a considerable length of time, it may in effect have simultaneously presented the truth in a fashion apparent only to the patient 'hairsplitter'.

Thus the Commission would still, in what may have been the only prudent and statesmanlike way, have lived up to its explicit duty of ascertaining and setting forth the facts. True, it would, in a way, have misled the public, yet only for a limited period of time - and furthermore only *that* segment of the public which was not going to the trouble of weighing every word published by, or through the agency of, the Commission. As it turned out, this segment was quite a substantial one...

Fourth and last, but not least: it is quite conceivable that this misleading of the public came about only as an unavoidable if regrettable corollary of what was possibly one of the chief intentions, if not even instructions, of the Commission: namely to *mislead above all the conspirators* (whoever they were) who had engineered and perpetrated the assassination.

As mentioned before, it follows from the incorrectness of the Warren Report's central thesis that there was a conspiracy. To this very date no authority has ever seen fit to identify this conspiracy, either as a body or as a collection of individual persons. Presumably it therefore was a powerful (domestic or foreign) one. Now if, as conjectured above, the full truth should indeed be hidden in the publications fathered by the Warren Commission, then we no longer need to speculate on why it should have been hidden there so deeply as to surrender only to hairsplitting analysis: the conspirators - or the persons dedicated to preventing their exposure - were to be kept as long as possible from making the panicking discovery that the Warren Commission, far from covering up their guilt, had in fact

---

[7] Epstein, op. cit.

brought it out into the open, be it in a most indirect and highly devious way.

If this was indeed what the Commission did, possibly even was instructed to do, then it is eminently logical and credible that it should have proceeded in the way as described: first serve the immediate 'national interest' by dispelling 'rumors and suspicions' and restoring 'the nation's faith in its institutions' in presenting its findings and conclusions in such a way that they at first, second and third glance permit only of lone killer Lee Harvey Oswald's single-handed guilt, thus simultaneously lulling the conspirators into false security and keeping them from any more desperate acts than individual killings of possibly damaging witnesses - while at the same time firmly ensuring that in the final analysis, only to be arrived at after numerous years of painstaking and 'hairsplitting' study, the full truth would be uncovered.

Should we be able to substantiate this hypothesis, then we will no longer be baffled by the question why seven men of the highest integrity and station signed a document which, if taken at face value, would make them go down into history as falsifiers of the truth. Nor will we wonder any longer why Robert F. Kennedy ever 'accepted' the Warren Report and declared himself 'completely satisfied' with it, nor why Pierre Salinger, without making any reference to Lee Harvey Oswald, had his belief put on record that 'the Warren Commission performed a difficult assignment honorably and well, and that it accurately pinpointed the assassin of John F. Kennedy.'

With these perspectives opening up, I trust the reader will bear with me if in the following chapters I invite him or her to join me in subjecting the Warren Report (in the widest sense) to a fair amount, and even more than that, of 'hairsplitting'.

III. The Instructions to the Warren Commission

The Warren Commission has been attacked by its critics for a variety of reasons: for picking the wrong assassin; for evolving 'political truth'[8] rather than presenting the actual facts; for devoting too little time to its task; for not permitting cross-examination of witnesses; for not hearing specific witnesses; for hearing others much too late; for not taking Jack Ruby to Washington when he implored to be taken there to tell the truth; for hardly conducting any independent investigations and chiefly relying on the FBI instead, etc. etc.

While by no means intimating that none of this criticism was to the point, I nevertheless would suggest that in all of it the main point was missed - the chief grounds on which the Commission's performance should be judged, the supreme standards by which its functioning and reporting should be measured.

The Commission had no mandate from, and was not answerable to, the public. It was a President's Commission, created by President Johnson to perform a specific task outlined by him in response to an obvious and pressing public need and laid down in precise instructions. In trying to determine whether the Commission performed its assignment well or badly, fairness alone dictates that we should measure it first of all, if not exclusively. by the terms of these instructions. Should we find that the Commission lived up to its instructions yet failed to perform a satisfactory job in the light of history, then our criticism should be directed primarily, if not exclusively, to the author of these instructions, i.e. President Johnson.

In judging on the Warren Commission, we must therefore first of all determine under what instructions it operated. Just what were they?

---

[8] Epstein, op. cit.

At least ever since the publication of the 'Warren Report' we have been familiar with these instructions well enough. Reproduced on its page 471 as Appendix I (and in the present book as Illustration 1) we find the text of President Johnson's 'Executive Order No. 11130' of November 29, 1963 spelling these instructions out. Now before looking at their detailed text let us first consider the interesting, if not indubitably established fact that this Executive Order, although a public document from the very beginning, having been handed out by the office of the White House Press Secretary (Pierre Salinger) on November 30, 1963 for immediate release, does not appear to have in fact become known to the public until the Warren Report was published.

To wit, I have not found any reference to Executive Order No. 11130, let alone any reprint of its full text, in the issues of the *New York Times* from November 29, 1963 onward, nor in the 1963 or 1964 volume of 'Facts on File', the well-known summarization of current affairs appearing from week to week in the USA. If these two instances should be typical, as they may well be, of the pertinent press coverage this would mean that all the time while the Commission was in function, hearing witnesses, gathering information, traveling all over the United States, preparing its final report, etc., the exact wording of its instructions, hence the precise nature of its mission, was unknown to the public.

Now there need not be anything sinister to this apparent failure of the media to publicize a document of capital importance. Under the circumstances the news value of the document appeared to be only slight, for on the preceding day, November 29, 1963, the office of the White House Press Secretary had issued another press release (reproduced as Appendix II to the Warren Report on its page 472 and as Illustration 2 to the present book) to which the next day's release seemed to add little if anything. This 283-word release of November 29 had announced the capital fact, a complete sensation at that moment, that President Johnson was appointing a Special Commission to investigate the Dallas events of a week ago; it had given the names of the members

18

of the Commission, described in detail the functions and powers of the nascent fact-finding body, and concluded with the most reassuring news that the President was instructing the Commission 'to report its findings and conclusions to him, to the American people, and the world.' Of course, this news completely dominated the front pages of the November 30, 1963 American press, which generally reprinted the full text of the White House release while also commenting on it in detail and printing at least a picture of Chief Justice Warren, the designated head of the Commission.

Now on the very day these papers were on the newsstands a new, slightly shorter (243 words) White House release gave the full text of the Executive Order by which the Special Commission was created and appointed, and its functions and powers laid down. In view of what the papers were full of anyway that day, none of this information, apparently a sheer rehashing of what was already known, seems to have been regarded by editors as having sufficient news value to crowd out any of the other post-assassination news still flooding them. Since, under the circumstances, not even the 'New York Times' appears to have regarded the Nov. 30 release as 'news fit to print', it is most unlikely that any other American newspaper, let alone foreign ones, did so regard it.

And yet a decisive point was missed in this way. To inaugurate, at this point, our hairsplitting, let us note that at least in one essential respect the official text of the President's instructions to his Special Commission did not duplicate his announcement of the previous day. *The Commission was not instructed, by Executive Order No. 11130, to report its findings and conclusions 'to the American people and to the world', but rather to the President alone.*

* *

*

This highly significant difference between the White House press releases of November 29 and 30, 1963 went completely unnoticed at the time - as well as later - by the American press, which admittedly had no

19

reason at that moment to indulge in hairsplitting. But neither had it reason, then or later, to misrepresent - however unwittingly - the facts, e.g. by reading into the November 29 release something which it decidedly did not say. This, however, was precisely what 'Facts on File' did when on page 424 of its 1963 volume it put the historic fact of the establishment of the Warren Commission on file as follows:

> 'President Johnson November 29 appointed a special commission headed by Chief Justice Earl Warren to investigate President Kennedy's assassination and the murder of his alleged assassin, Lee Harvey Oswald. The White House said Mr. Johnson had instructed the commission "to satisfy itself that the truth is known as far as it can be discovered and to report its findings and conclusions to him, to the American people, and to the world".'

Obviously, this account of the facts (and 'Facts on File' just stands here for numerous other publications) was based on the White House release of November 29 rather than on that of the next day with the precise, official text of the President's instructions. Thus it constituted in itself a piece of unprecise reporting. But even more important: the November 29 release was *quoted incorrectly*. The release had not said that Mr. Johnson *had instructed* the Commission 'to report its findings and conclusions to ... the American people and to the world,' it rather said that he *was so instructing it* - which, to a hairsplitter, is an entirely different statement.

In fact, it would have been completely impossible for the White House release of November 29 to employ the past tense and say that the President *had* given the Commission certain instructions. To be given instructions, a commission must first of all *exist*. Now throughout its text the press release assumes that the President's Commission is only in the process of being created and does not yet in fact exist. It starts out by saying: 'The President today announced that he *is appointing* (italics mine, J.Z.) a Special Commission...', refers to it in the next paragraph as 'the *proposed* Special Commission' and later dwells on how 'the Special Commission *is to be* instructed'. Logically speaking, therefore, we cannot with absolute certainly infer from the November 29 release under what Presidential instructions the Warren Commission actually operated.

What we *can* say for sure on the grounds of the two White House press releases of November 29 and 30, 1963 - provided we take both of them at face value, as I shall do here, unwilling as I find myself to join the ranks of those who suspect a President of the United States and a truth-finding body appointed by him of lying, if not even of worse - is the following:

1. At some time on November 29, 1963, preceding the drafting of the White House press release and the Executive Order of that date, President Johnson was phrasing instructions to his proposed Special Commission telling it to find out as much of the truth as it or anyone could, and to report this truth to him, to the American people, and to the world.
2. Of these instructions, the Executive Order signed by the President at some later time that same day incorporates those telling the Commission to find out as much of the truth as it or anyone could, and to report this truth to him, the President.

Now from these two incontrovertible facts we are forced to conclude that:

either: President Johnson at some time on November 29 - a time succeeding the announcement of the White House press release of that date but preceding the drafting of Executive Order No. 11130-reconsidered his intention of instructing the Special Commission to tell the truth also to the American people and to the world, without, however, making his change of mind publicly known on that or any later date;

or: President Johnson did indeed instruct the Special Commission to tell the truth also to the American people and to the world, but these instructions were contained, possibly together with various other ones, in a special Executive Order, so far unpublished and unknown, or in special, secret clauses of Executive Order No. 11130, or in some other confidential message to the Commission.

Now are we in a position to decide which of the two alternatives mentioned conforms to the truth? We are indeed, for we know at least *some* of the things the Commission has done in fulfillment of whatever instructions it had, in the aggregate, received from the President. We know that on September 24, 1964 it presented to the President the 888-page document generally known as the 'Warren Report' (and in this book to be generally referred to under that name). Now thanks to the invaluable efforts of the critics of the Warren Report we know beyond a doubt that this report did by no means contain 'the truth as far as it can be discovered' or anything even approaching it. Anyone begging to differ here should stop reading the present book at this point at the latest and start doing something he apparently has omitted so far: study the Warren Report, preferably in conjunction with any of the numerous and competent work by the critics.

Now from the inadequacy of the Warren Report I am not going to draw the conclusion inferred - explicitly or implicitly - by not a few assassination students in the past, namely that either President Johnson acted in bad faith when instructing the Commission to find out the truth (while actually wanting it to cover it up), or that the bad faith was on the part of the Commission, which, although instructed to ascertain the truth, in fact came up with a cover-up story. In both cases we would be dealing with dishonorable, or at best with cowardly men - an assumption no one should make unless absolutely compelled to do so.

In this case there is no question of such compulsion. For both the existence and the untruthfulness of the Warren Report can be fully explained, and the integrity of both President Johnson and his Special Commission preserved, by assuming that the second one of the two alternatives presented on pages 19 and 20 is true, hence that the Commission received from the President, besides Executive Order No. 11130, *additional instructions,* which to accountfor every inconsistency unsolved so far must have comprised at least the following ones:

1. to write, in addition to a truthful report pursuant to Executive Order No. 11130, a further report in the nature of the 'Warren Report';
2. to report the truth 'to the American people and to the world' in some other form than in that of an explicit document spelling it out in detail.

These two points sum up the substance of what I have been able to learn about the Warren Commission's instructions from the White House press releases of November 29 and 30, 1963. I admit it is not much. But we can go on from here. We shall do so by now turning to other extraneous parts of the Warren Report than its Appendices I and II. The Report itself, bearing not much of a relation as it does to the truth, will not interest us in this book.

IV.   The Warren Report's Nimble Self-Exposure

As I have come to discover, prolonged critical preoccupation with the publications of the Warren Commission may make one sufficiently versed in the art of hairsplitting to solve the mystery of the Warren Report from a mere look at its title page. If the reader is kind enough to stay with me until the end of this chapter he will by then have attained this pinnacle.

At the present moment, however, I must ask him to turn over the Report's title page and to look instead at a further page preceding its actual body - namely the brief (four-line) letter, signed by all 7 Commissioners, by which the Commission submitted the 'Warren Report' to President Johnson. For all its brevity, this letter is a hairsplitter's dream. It is shown in this book as Illustration 3.

As in the case of 'Appendix I' discussed in the previous chapter we will first leave the body of the letter alone and devote our attention to its peripheral aspects, the chief one of which, of course, is the lofty collection of autographs beneath it, not, to my knowledge, found duplicated anywhere else in, or in connection with, the Warren Report. This 'Letter of Transmittal', then, supposedly is the document expressing the 7 Commissioners' unanimous endorsement of the Warren Report, the crowning of Mr. Warren's efforts to present, despite any reluctance or resistance on the part of this or that Commissioner, a unanimous Report.

Now just what was there to this letter that may have made it so difficult to sign for one or another Commissioner, thus making for such a dramatic 'battle for unanimity'? Just what does the precious letter say? Let us quote it verbatim - it's not much of a job:

'Dear Mr. President:
    Your Commission to investigate the assassination of President

Kennedy on November 22, 1963, having completed its assignment in accordance with Executive Order No. 11130 of November 29, 1963, herewith submits its final report.

Respectfully,
....................,

In effect, then, the Commissioners here jointly and severally assert just two things to be true:

1. They have completed their assignment in accordance with Executive Order No. 11130.
2. They are now, on September 24, 1964, submitting their final report.

Now one feels inclined to wonder what on earth there may have been to battle about in these two assertions. Surely the Commission, on the verge of going out of existence, must have considered its assignment as completed, and surely the 'Warren Report' was its final report - sheer lack of time would have prevented the writing of an additional one. The alleged battle for unanimity[9] would have made more sense if assertion 2 had been amplified to end e.g. as follows: '...its final report, which in the sincere opinion of all of the undersigned does indeed present the truth as far as it can be discovered.'

Of course one might take the view that this latter supplementary statement was implicitly contained in the Commission's assertion '1' with its reference to Executive Order No. 11130, from which the added statement is a paraphrased quotation. But this view would be erroneous - even a modest amount of hairsplitting suffices to render it totally untenable.

Let us look quite carefully at the *precise* text of the Commission's Letter of Transmittal in the light of the *precise* text of Executive Order No. 11130. Or, to narrow this task down: let us jointly consider the

---

[9] Cf. e.g. Epstein, op. cit., chapter 10.

Commission's assertion that it had completed its assignment under Executive Order No. 11130 and the instruction to the Commission, contained *inter alia* in this Executive Order, to report its findings and conclusions to the President.

We then see that, strictly and hence correctly speaking, the Commission could not possibly have stated *at any time* that it had completed its assignment under Executive Order No. 11130 unless *at that time* it *had* already reported 'the truth as far as it can be discovered' to the President. For this reporting job formed an essential component of the Commission's complex overall assignment under that Executive Order.

This entire argument would of course crumble if the Commission's Letter of Transmittal had read just a little bit different - if it had said, for example, that the Commission, *in order to complete* its assignment under Executive Order No. 11130, now submits its final report - or that it herewith submits its final report, *thereby completing* its assignment in accordance with Executive Order No. 11130. However, the letter of course cannot read any other way than it does. Aware, therefore, of this wording of the Commission's Letter of Transmittal, remembering the calibre, station and lawyer minds of the men who signed it, and giving a fair amount of credence to the rumors and reports that they labored hard (even 'battled') to frame it just right, we can draw only one, but momentous conclusion:

> When the Commissioners, on September 24, 1964, signed their Letter of Transmittal to President Johnson, they *had at that moment already reported the truth about the assassination*, to the extent that they had ascertained it, to the President. This they must therefore have done in *another* report than the Warren Report made public on September 28, 1964.

*　　*

*

As I remarked a moment ago, this conclusion is a momentous one, and it is therefore fortunate that we immediately find it corroborated in the same four-line Letter of Transmittal we are analyzing here, namely where the Commission says it is herewith submitting its *'final report'*.

For unless the Warren Report followed some *other* report or reports there of course would have been no need, nor any reason for the Commission to call this document its *final* report. Both logic and linguistics tell us therefore that there must have been at least one further report by the Warren Commission, antedating or at least preceding its 'Warren Report'.

This is also confirmed by American government usage as we know it. Thus the next Presidential Commission created by President Johnson, the one on Heart Disease, Cancer and Stroke (established on March 7, 1964; chairman: Dr. Michael E. De Bakey), when presenting its report started out its letter of transmittal, signed by its chairman, with the words: 'Dear Mr. President: I have the honor to submit *the report* of the President's Commission...'. Likewise, the letter by which President Kennedy's Commission on the Status of Women submitted to him, on October 11, 1963, its report started out thus: 'Dear Mr. President: In presenting to you *the report* of your Commission...' (italics mine, J.Z.), In both cases only one report was submitted (although in the former case in two volumes), and it was referred to as 'the report', not 'the final report', of the pertinent Commission.

In contrast, the Department of Health, Education and Welfare's 'Task Force on Prescription Drugs' on February 7, 1969 presented the Secretary of the Department its 'Final Report', the title page of which is reproduced as our Illustration 4. But here this report was indeed preceded by several (five, to be exact) other reports, as is evident from its Letter of Transmittal as shown on our Illustration 5 (on which the underlinings are mine, J.Z.).

All along the line, therefore, we find nothing but support for our assumption of at least one further report by the Warren Commission, which, to distinguish it from the ill-famed 'Warren Report', we shall as of now call the 'Commission Report'. Now what can we say of this Commission Report? There are at least three aspects of it we would like to know more about, namely: (1) its contents, (2)   the date and manner of its presentation to the President, and (3)   its size. Now interestingly, although the existence of this Commission Report has so far only been deduced, not officially confirmed, we can give fairly concrete information on all three aspects.

First as to its *contents*: Executive Order No. 11130 instructed the Commission to ascertain the truth and report it to the President. As we know, the Warren Report does not contain whatever truth the Commission ascertained (and considering its powers, the Commission presumably ascertained all there was to ascertain). This truth must therefore have been set forth in the 'Commission Report', thus making it a most vital, intriguing and historic document.

Next as to the *date* of the 'Commission Report' or at least of its presentation: here we have a most interesting clue in an official document so far unconsidered in this analysis: the official photograph of the presentation, by Chief Justice Warren, of the Warren Commission's report to President Johnson on September 24, 1964, shown as Illustration 6 of this book.

Evidently, Mr. Warren is presenting President Johnson a volume of momentous size. Since the 'Warren Report' as we know it had not yet been made public at that time, no- one was of course in a position to note that the report volume as photographed was far more voluminous than the 'Warren Report' published a few days later.

The difference between both volumes is quite substantial and can in fact be precisely determined. The 'Warren Report', as everyone in possession of it can verify, is exactly 2 inches thick. Given the positions of Messrs. Johnson and Warren in the famous picture and their respective sizes (with the then President of course towering above his Chief Justice), the presentation scene can be readily reconstructed and the thickness of the volume changing hands precisely measured, especially since all of its edges are visible (although in one instance only barely; here one might almost speak of visual hairsplitting). While not having performed such a reconstruction myself, I am entirely sure even without it that the volume visible in the picture is quite appreciably thicker than 2 inches.

This second-hand personal impression, which I presume anyone else will likewise obtain when studying the picture, is entirely in agreement with the first-hand impression gained by the New York Times reporter present at the presentation scene:

> ' "It's pretty heavy," said President Johnson, as the boxed, Navy blue, four-inch thick volume - about the size of Who's Who - was handed to him by Mr. Warren. Those were the only clear words reporters could overhear.'[10]

The reporter's estimate of four inches surpasses my personal guess by approx. one inch, but in any event it is clear that the covers of the 'presentation volume' must have enclosed appreciably more than the 888 pages of the 'Warren Report' released four days later.

One might assume, of course, that the special volume presented to President Johnson included also the special, sensitive information which Chairman Warren had said would be made public only years after the assassination (75 years, as President Johnson later precised it) - and if this material should account for the entire difference in thickness, then it obviously is quite voluminous. But it is equally possible, and in my opinion much more likely, that the 'presentation volume' visible on the official photograph of the 'ceremony' consisted of:

1. the 'Commission Report', setting forth the truth 'as far as it can be discovered', plus
2. the 'Warren Report' as we know it and as it was made public four days later,
   both bound together in a single volume.

This would, by all standards, be the most simple solution. For the 'Commission Report' must at some time have been submitted to President Johnson, this reporting of the truth having been after all the kernel of the

---

[10] The New York Times, issue of September 25, 1964.

President's Executive Order No. 11130. Now we know of no other occasion on which President Johnson might have been handed a Warren Commission report by its chairman or any other Commissioner. Furthermore the 'Commission Report', presenting the unvarnished and complete truth, would auto-matically have incorporated the aspects to he released only 75 years later, so that we need look for no further opportunity for a presentation of this latter material.

Finally, to split hairs again, the presentation of both the 'Commission' and the 'Warren Report' on the same occasion is wholly compatible, strange though it may seem, with the text of the Warren Report's Letter of Transmittal. This letter, one will recall, stated *inter alia* that the Commission had (already) met its obligations under Executive Order No. 11130, hence had already reported its findings and conclusions to the President. In effect, however, under my assumption, these findings and conclusions were handed over to the President *simultaneously* with the letter stating that they had already been reported. So?

To a seasoned hairsplitter this problem presents no difficulties whatsoever. He will e.g. remark that 'to report' a thing (i.e. to write a report on it, to address this report to the proper person and to put it into the proper channel) and 'to submit a report' on it (which may mean the physical act of handing over the report) need not be the same thing. The latter is what Mr. Warren did on September 24, 1964 - but the reporting had been done by the entire Commission before then. This seems to solve the problem, but actually it begs the question, for all this is true of the 'Warren Report', too.

More to the point is the following argument: the Letter of Trans-mittal (our Illustration 3) was predated in any event, for its date, September 24, 1964, is the one on which Mr. Warren handed President Johnson the bound volume incorporating this very letter. Obviously then, this letter had been written and signed *prior* to September 24; its date must be viewed in the light of when it was *presented to,* and its contents in the light of when it was *read by* its recipient, i.e. President Johnson.

Now since in the bound presentation volume the 'Warren Report', being the Commission's 'final report', must have *followed* the 'Commission

30

Report', it is obvious that President Johnson, when in his perusal of the gargantuan combined volume 'hitting' on the Warren Report's Letter of Transmittal, must *already have waded through the 'Commission Report'* prepared under his Executive Order No. 11130. Thus, it would have been strictly in order for him to be informed at that point that the Commission had 'completed its assignment in accordance with' the aforementioned Executive Order. Anyone placing himself into the then President's position will agree that there is nothing whatever improper about this procedure.

*   *

*

Third: as to the *size* of the 'Commission Report'. If we remain with Mr. Johnson a little longer we will find the answer to this third question as well (discovering in so doing that the ex-President is an accomplished hairsplitter himself).

To this end we need go back into history just a few months: to early 1970 when Walter Cronkite interviewed Mr. Johnson for his TV series 'LBJ, Tragedy and Transition'. In the 2nd interview, telecast on February 6,1970, Mr. Johnson declared (as retranslated by me from the Dutch):

> 'To come back to the (November 1963) Texas trip, Walter, I must say that a great deal has been written about it. As far as my personal knowledge goes, most of it is wrong, and purposely wrong at that.'[11]

Mr. Johnson undoubtedly was correct all around. A great deal has indeed been written about the John F. Kennedy assassination, the chief event, of course, of the 'Texas trip'. Now how far does one suppose ex-President Johnson's personal knowledge of this literature goes? Would he, with practically unlimited sources of information at his disposal, have ever found it necessary to read the works - however revealing to the

---

[11] De Volkskrant, Amsterdam, April 30, 1970.

average citizen - of the Commission's critics? The question is ridiculous. President Johnson had his 'Warren Report' and his 'Commission Report', and he knew better than any critic that the former was a mere construction, so why should he waste his time reading books telling him just that?

Mr. Johnson's personal knowledge may thus be assumed to be limited to the Warren Report and the Commission Report, of which the former is 'wrong, and purposely wrong at that'. Properly read, therefore, Mr. Johnson's statement informs us that the truthful 'Commission Report' is shorter than the untruthful 'Warren Report'.

Thus, we have so far established, with full or near-certainty, the following facts about our assumed, truthful and complete 'Commission Report':

1. It exists.
2. It sets forth 'the truth as far as it can be discovered' and it was submitted to President Johnson, both in accordance with Executive Order No. 11130.
3. It was bound together with the 'Warren Report' into a single volume, shown on the presentation ceremony photograph.
4. Within that volume, it preceded the Warren Report.
5. It was shorter than the Warren Report.

Now in addition to all this we can say three further things about the 'Commission Report'. We know what its *title page* must have looked like; we know that it also exists as a *separate volume*; and possibly we are even roughly familiar with its *Table of Contents*.

As to *the title page*: the Commission Report was prepared in compliance with Executive Order No. 11130. It is therefore only logical to assume that on its title page it contained exactly the same detailed reference to this Executive Order as is found on that of *each one of the* 26 volumes of Hearings and Exhibits (see Illustration 7).

The remainder of the Commission Report's title page may well - except for one further detail - have been wholly identical to that of the Warren Report (shown in Illustration 8), which, conspicuously, does *not* refer to

Executive Order No. 11130. An omission which is wholly in order, for the Warren Report could of course not possibly be announced as a document prepared *'Pursuant to (an) Executive Order'* calling for maximum possible truthfulness.

The *title itself,* however, of the Commission Report - and this is the detail meant above - is not wholly identical to that of the Warren Report, the 'Report of the President's Commission on the Assassination of President *John F.* Kennedy' (italics mine, J.Z.). Instead, it omits the words 'John F.', as we know from the last sentence - a sentence also informing us of the existence of a *separate volume* of the Commission Report - of the first paragraph of the Foreword to Volume I of the Hearings, a volume bearing the quality seal of truth in its reference to Executive Order No. 11130:

> 'The findings of the Commission, based on an examination of all the facts, are set forth in the separate volume entitled "Report of the President's Commission on the Assassination of President Kennedy".'

The latter designation of the Commission is indeed the proper, correct, and official one, as any of the numerous official references, past and present, to the Commission will confirm. Strictly and -under the circumstances - hence correctly speaking, therefore, the Warren Report presented itself as a report by a Commission which, under that name, did not even exist.

To a hair-splitter, ergo - to revert to what was said at the beginning of this chapter - the title page of the Warren Report, for all its brevity, is a most revealing document. Seldom, indeed, in the history of governmental investigation has so much been told to so many in so few words.

And finally as to the Commission Report's possible *Table of Contents:* this we find summed up in the last section, fittingly called 'The Commission's Report', of the official Foreword to the Warren Report.

Here, of course, we have to be careful. If the untruthfulness of the Warren Report extends to its Foreword as well, then we would merely waste our time even looking at it. But if the Foreword is one of the 'peripheral documents' containing essential clues we would be fools to dismiss it out of hand. Now to judge by what is said on its many pages preceding the final section discussed here, the Foreword may well be marked by truth throughout. Li this case the Report it discusses is the truthful Commission Report, as is evident from the first sentences of this section:

> *'The Commission's Report.*
> In this report the Commission submits the results of its investigation. Each member of the Commission has given careful consideration to the entire report and concurs in its find-ings and conclusions...'

What follows then would therefore be a tantalizing, if partial summary of the unpublished, truthful Report:

> '...The report consists of an initial chapter summarizing the Commission's basic findings and conclusions, followed by a detailed analysis of the facts and the issues raised by the events of November 22, 1963, and the 2 following days. Individual chapters consider the trip to Dallas, the shots from the Texas School Book Depository, the identity of the assassin, the killing of Lee Harvey Oswald, the possibility of a conspiracy, Oswald's background and possible motive, and arrangements for the protection of the President...'

Even a truthful Report may of course well have contained chapters on these subjects - in addition to, say, chapters on the shots from the grassy knoll, the true killers' backgrounds and indubitable motives, etc. A clue suggesting that the above is indeed (part of) a summary of a true report's table of contents is the word 'possible' applied to Oswald's motive, as a 'possible' motive on Oswald's part is the only one a true report could have discussed, undoubtedly to reach the conclusion that where there is no deed there can be no motive.

Of equal interest to the hairsplitter is the reference to a chapter on 'the identity of the assassin'. How could a true report speak of 'the assassin' where in fact there were several? It could by taking the position that the only real, i.e. successful assassin was the person firing the lethal headshot. That there were in reality two, near-simultaneous head shots (hence two actual assassins), as ably and ingeniously established by such Warren Report critics as Philadelphia lawyer Vincent J. Salandria and Haverford professor Jo-siah Thompson,[12] might escape even a genuinely truth-seeking Commission. But if the above analysis is correct, this Commission did then at least establish, in its truthful Commission Report, the identity of *one* of these killers. In this Report the Commission must thus indeed have 'named names' - and presumably supplied the evidence.

---

[12] Josiah Thompson: *'Six Seconds in Dallas'*, chapter V.

V. Cryptographic Truth

All of our findings so far were obtained through a precise analysis of just a few peripheral aspects of the Warren Report wholly extraneous to its body of information, namely: its title page, its Foreword, its Letter of Transmittal, its Appendices I and II (1-page documents each), and the photograph of its official presentation. Yet this scanty information has permitted us to entirely revolutionize the consensus of opinion as to what the Warren Report is about.

Now this, I submit, is decidedly not by chance. I am convinced that all of these clues were purposely built into the Warren Report in accordance with President Johnson's aforementioned secret instructions which also account for the writing of the Warren Report as such.

It was in this manner that the Commission was able to escape, even transcend, its dilemma so aptly described by Epstein:

> 'There was... a dualism in purpose. If the explicit purpose of the Commission was to ascertain and expose the facts, the implicit purpose was to protect the national interest by dispelling rumors.
> 'These two purposes were compatible so long as the damaging rumors were untrue. But what if a rumor damaging to the national interest proved to be true? The Commission's explicit purpose would dictate that the information be exposed regard-less of the consequences, while the Commission's implicit purpose would dictate that the rumor be dispelled regardless of the fact that it was true. In a conflict of this sort, one of the Commission's purposes would emerge as dominant.'[13]

In other words, Epstein says that the Commission, faced with a two-horned dilemma, would decide in favor of one of the horns -and in his next sub-chapter, 'The Dilemma' (of whether the Commission should risk

---

[13] Epstein, op. cit., chapter 2: 'The Dominant Purpose'.

exposing Oswald as an FBI informer or not), Epstein makes it plain that in his opinion the Commission decided in favor of its 'implicit purpose', thus making the 'protection of the national interest' its dominant goal.

Mr. Epstein's argument is valid and his example is to the point, yet the possibility did not occur to him that the Commission, with all the brain power at its disposal, might have tried to rise above its dilemma and serve both its explicit and implicit purpose at the same time.

This, I have found, is exactly what the Commission did. In a wonderfully dialectical way it explicitly honored its implicit purpose (meaning that the Warren Report served the 'national interest' rather than the truth) while implicitly honoring its explicit one (meaning that the truth - explicitly spelled out in the Commission Report for the President's eyes only - is implicitly contained in the Warren Commission's published information.)

At this point it is appropriate to say two further things regarding Mr. Epstein's research and his lucid argumentation.

First, in making a discovery which escaped Mr. Epstein although he was quite close to it I merely took over the torch from him. Mr. Epstein, through painstaking research no doubt, exposed the merely 'political' truthfulness of the Warren Report. Thanks to him and his fellow-critics I therefore did not have to bother (and in fact 'am none too familiar) with it. I did examine it from one particular point of view and found it to be, in this particular respect, a complete fabrication. This convinced me that anything critical anyone has ever said of the Warren Report is most probably true.

Second: It might be easily followed from Mr. Epstein's correct analysis that it was not considered in the American national interest to disclose the truth about President Kennedy's assassination, which was therefore most likely a product of an American conspiracy. Let me hasten to say that this would be a most irresponsible instance of jumping to conclusions.

For example: it would emphatically be against the American national interest if an international crisis were conjured up where none was called for. Now suppose, just speculating, that there was not an *American*, but an *international* (as first conjectured) or at least a *foreign* conspiracy behind the assassination - but not one for which, say, the Russian or Cuban official government was to blame. Let us say the Soviet KGB, employing e.g. Oswald as its puppet, had launched a solo operation to eliminate a foreign statesman it hated and to put an end to an international development (e.g. budding Soviet-American rapprochement) it considered dangerous to Russia - *and that all this was known* to the American government when the Warren Commission started its work, or became known in the course of it.

Obviously it might then very well have been in 'the American national interest' to soft-pedal the entire affair, to prevent an international crisis, to give the possibly wholly innocent 'visible' Soviet government the time to purge its 'invisible' one and to have a halfway plausible alternative account of the assassination written up. - The aforegoing was just a model; dozens like it might be thought up in the nuclear age. Clearly there is more to the national interest than the protection of certain domestic institutions.

This said, let us turn now to the Warren Commission's implicit uncovering of the truth. Just where did it do so? One possible answer would be: in the Warren Report. The Report is 888 pages long, so that a vast body of truth may be written between its lines.

Yet this possibility must be rejected for various reasons. The lacking reference to Executive Order No. 11130 suggests that the Report bears no relation, explicit or implicit, to the truth. Hundreds of historians, researchers, editors, authors, etc. have subjected the Report to closest scrutiny, and - with one exception - have failed to unearth instances of 'writing between the lines' identifiable by hairsplitting analysis. (The one exception is the Report's conspicuous preference - singled out by Harold *Weisberg*[14] - for speaking of the 'shooting' rather than the 'murder' or the 'killing' of Oswald by Ruby, a preference looking like a hidden clue in view of the fact that Oswald undoubtedly was only *wounded*, possibly not even lethally, by Ruby's bullet, with the lethal effects subsequently being brought on by the vigorous artificial respiration to which Oswald was immediately subjected by an unidentified 'detective',[15] Yet this lone,

---

[14] Harold Weisberg: *'Whitewash'*, chapter 8.
[15] Cf. the account of this episode in William Manchester: *'The Death of a President'* (a document possibly likewise susceptible of rewarding hairsplitting analysis).

38

anything but consistent example cannot qualify this Report as a pearl of hidden truth.) And finally: the various clues we have detected in the peripheral documents of the Warren Report, though telling us the truth about this Report, tell us nothing about the truth about the assassination.

Now if it was not in the Warren Report, then the Commission must have hidden - and indeed did hide - this truth in its 26 Volumes of Hearings and Exhibits, on whose 20,000-odd pages the Commission carried the art of writing between the lines to an unprecedented and indeed unbelievable height.

This was the discovery gradually but inescapably imposing itself on me when in the past few years I examined the 'Warren Report' in conjunction with the '26 Volumes' from one specific, to me most intriguing point of view, which need not be discussed here as the present booklet is an 'Invitation to Hairsplitting' rather than an exhibition of hairs already split. Suffice it to say that it bears no direct relation to any of the three Dallas murders. I find it more to the point to remark that well-known Commission critic Mark *Lane*[16] a few years ago came within a hair's breadth of hitting on the true function of the Warren Commission and the true nature of its '26 Volumes' when citing from the latter[17] the following description given, under oath, by Mrs. Helen Markham of her 'identification', in a lineup at Dallas Police headquarters, of Oswald as the killer of Officer Tippit - a killer of whom she assured Commissioner Allen W. Dulles: *'I would know the man anywhere, I know I would,'*[18]

> *Q.:* Now when you went into the room you looked these people over, these four men?
> *Markham:* Yes, sir.
> *Q.:* Did you recognize anyone in the lineup?
> *Markham:* No, sir.
> *Q.:* You did not? Did you see anybody - I have asked you
> that question before - did you recognize anybody from their

---

[16] In *'Rush to Judgment'*, chapter 14.
[17] Hearings and Exhibits, 3 H 310 (Helen *Markham*).
[18] Ibid., 3 H 312.

face?

Markham: From their face, no.

Q.: Did you identify anybody in these four people?

Markham: I didn't know nobody.

Q.: I know you didn't know anybody, but did anybody in that lineup look like anybody you had seen before?

Markham: No. I had never seen none of them, none of these men.

Q.: No one of the four?

Markham: No one of them.

Q.: No one of all four?

Markham: No, sir.

The No. 2 man in this lineup was Lee Harvey Oswald.

With this 'hair', not much of a one to split, the reader is kindly invited to start his own hairsplitting, thus discovering for himself the cryptographic - rather than explicit or 'political' - truth set forth by the Warren Commission.

Illustrations

(1-8)

(Underlinings and framings by the author)

APPENDIX I

Office of the White House Press Secretary

- -

THE WHITE HOUSE

EXECUTIVE ORDER
NO.11130
- - - -

APPOINTING A COMMISSION TO REPORT UPON THE
ASSASSINATION OF PRESIDENT JOHN F. KENNEDY

Pursuant to the authority vested in me as President of the United States, I hereby appoint a Commission to ascertain, evaluate and report upon the facts relating to the assassination of the late President John F. Kennedy and the subsequent violent death of the man charged with the assassination. The Commission shall consist of --

The Chief Justice of the United States, Chairman;

Senator Richard B. Russell;

Senator John Sherman Cooper;

Congressman Hale Boggs;

Congressman Gerald R. Ford;

The Honorable Allen W. Dulles;

The Honorable John J. McCloy.

The purposes of the Commission are to examine the evidence developed by the Federal Bureau of Investigation and any additional evidence that may hereafter come to light or be uncovered by federal or state authorities; to make such further investigation as the Commission finds desirable; to evaluate all the facts and circumstances surrounding such assassination, including the subsequent violent death of the man charged with the assassination, and to report to me its findings and conclusions.

The Commission is empowered to prescribe its own procedures and to employ such assistants as it deems necessary.

Necessary expenses of the Commission may be paid from the "Emergency Fund for the President".

All Executive departments and agencies are directed to furnish the Commission with such facilities, services and cooperation as it may request from time to time.

LYNDON B. JOHNSON

THE WHITE HOUSE,

November 29, 1963.

* * *

Ill. 1

APPENDIX II

<pre>
IMMEDIATE RELEASE   November 29, 1963

          Office of the White House Press Secretary
- -
</pre>

THE WHITE HOUSE

The President today announced that he is appointing a Special Commission to study and report upon all facts and circumstances relating to the assassination of the late President, John F. Kennedy, and the subsequent violent death of the man charged with the assassination.

The President stated that the Majority and Minority Leadership of the Senate and the House of Representatives have been consulted with respect to the proposed Special Commission.

The members of the Special Commission are:

> Chief Justice Earl Warren, Chairman
> Senator Richard Russell (Georgia)
> Senator John Sherman Cooper (Kentucky)
> Representative Hale Boggs (Louisiana)
> Representative Gerald Ford (Michigan)
> Hon. Allen W. Dulles of Washington
> Hon. John J. McCloy of New York

The President stated that the Special Commission is to be instructed to evaluate all available information concerning the subject of the inquiry. The Federal Bureau of Investigation, pursuant to an earlier directive of the President, is making complete investigation of the facts. An inquiry is also scheduled by a Texas Court of Inquiry convened by the Attorney General of Texas under Texas law.

The Special Commission will have before it all evidence uncovered by the Federal Bureau of Investigation and all information available to any agency of the Federal Government. The Attorney General of Texas has also offered his cooperation. All Federal agencies and offices are being directed to furnish services and cooperation to the Special Commission. The Commission will also be empowered to conduct any further investigation that it deems desirable.

The President is instructing the Special Commission to satisfy itself that the truth is known as far as it can be discovered, and to report its findings and conclusions to him, to the American people, and to the world.

#####

Ill. 2

September 24, 1964

The President
The White House
Washington, D. C.

Dear Mr. President:

Your Commission to investigate the assassination of President Kennedy on November 22, 1963, having completed its assignment in accordance with Executive Order No. 11130 of November 29, 1963, herewith submits its final report.

Respectfully,

Earl Warren, Chairman

Richard B. Russell

John Sherman Cooper

Hale Boggs

Gerald R. Ford

Allen W. Dulles

John J. McCloy

Ill. 3

TASK FORCE ON PRESCRIPTION DRUGS

FINAL REPORT

February 7, 1969

Office of the Secretary

U.S. DEPARTMENT OF HEALTH, EDUCATION, AND WELFARE

Washington, D.C. 20201

III. 4

Task Force on Prescription Drugs - <u>Final Report</u>

"In May of 1967, upon a directive from the President,
the Task Force on Prescription Drugs was established
to undertake a comprehensive study of the problems
of including the costs of prescription drugs under
Medicare.

During the ensuing 20 months, the Task Force carried
out a number of studies involved in this complex
assignment. Based on this work, <u>we have already
completed and submitted five interim reports.</u>

<u>I am now pleased to transmit for your consideration
the final report,</u> which summarizes the major findings
and recommendations previously included in the
interim reports. Perhaps the most significant are
these:

Ill. 5

Ill. 6

INVESTIGATION OF
THE ASSASSINATION OF PRESIDENT JOHN F. KENNEDY

HEARINGS

Before the President's Commission

on the Assassination

of President Kennedy

PURSUANT TO EXECUTIVE ORDER 11130, an Executive order creating a Commission to ascertain, evaluate, and report upon the facts relating to the assassination of the late President John F. Kennedy and the subsequent violent death of the man charged with the assassination and S.J. RES. 137, 88TH CONGRESS, a concurrent resolution conferring upon the Commission the power to administer oaths and affirmations, examine witnesses, receive evidence, and issue subpenas

Volume

III

UNITED STATES GOVERNMENT PRINTING OFFICE

WASHINGTON, D.C.

III. 7

REPORT OF
THE PRESIDENT'S COMMISSION ON THE
ASSASSINATION OF
President John F. Kennedy

UNITED STATES

GOVERNMENT PRINTING OFFICE

WASHINGTON, D.C.

Ill. 8